Stopping on the Bridge

Stopping on the Bridge

Poems by

Dianne Woods Ashley

© 2022 Dianne Woods Ashley. All rights reserved.
This material may not be reproduced in any form, published,
reprinted, recorded, performed, broadcast,
rewritten or redistributed without
the explicit permission of Dianne Woods Ashley.
All such actions are strictly prohibited by law.

Cover design by Shay Culligan
Cover art by Heather Pilchard

ISBN: 978-1-63980-199-2

Kelsay Books
502 South 1040 East, A-119
American Fork, Utah 84003
Kelsaybooks.com

*To my parents,
Virginia Woods Ashley,
who loved Cape Cod,
and Robert Paul Ashley,
who loved words
and literature*

Acknowledgments

Grateful acknowledgement to the editors of the following journals, anthologies, and newspapers where these poems first appeared, sometimes in different versions and with different titles:

Brewster Ladies Library, Poem of the month: "The Women's House," "Edward Hopper's Cape Cod Evening," "Inside a Frame of Leaves"

Cape Cod Cultural Center Poetry Contest, judged by Tony Hoagland: Honorable Mention in the national category: "Some Advice If You Want to Go to a Peace Vigil"

Cape Cod Times: "April Birthday," "Eritrea," "Kneel down," "Pilgrimage to Race Point"

Great River Review: "The Baby from Another World"

Metropolitan: "Embryo"

Passager, Honorable Mention in 2019: "The Women's House"

Poems Against War, An Anthology: "The Courage of Boys"

Potomac Review: "Early Morning in Pocasset"

Virginia Writing: "Two Backyards," "Snow Writing"

Voices of Peace, the Cape Cod Veterans for Peace annual poetry competition and magazine: "1601 Pennsylvania Avenue," "Witness in Sheikh Jarrah, East Jerusalem," "Some Advice If You Want to Go to a Peace Vigil"

WOMR Joe Gouveia Annual Poetry Contest, judged by Marge Piercy*:* "The Women's House," won Third Place and "Animal Nights," "The Unknown Migrant," "Turning Compost" won Honorable Mention

I am grateful to the poets in my first writing group at the Writers' Center in Bethesda, Maryland including Ebby Malmgren, Davi Waters, and Jane Weiner. Also to my first poetry teacher on Cape Cod—June Beisch, and the students in her class, including Diane Hanna, Pam Foss, and Lee Kane.

Many teachers and students at the Fine Arts Work Center in Provincetown and Castle Hill Center for the Arts inspired me to write, and revise the poems in this book: Brenda Shaughnessy, Dorianne Laux, Cleopatra Mathis, Maxine Kumin, David Baker, and especially Daisy Fried. At the Wellfleet Library, Rosalind Pace and Alan Friedman led helpful workshops.

Peter Campion, who has taught at both Castle Hill and the Fine Arts Work Center, is teacher and mentor par excellence. He is responsible for inspiring the best poems in this book and bringing the manuscript to fruition.

Much thanks to Marge Piercy for her unique and generous workshop and for inviting me into her poetry group. Thanks to the members of the group for feedback: Lucile Burt, Elaine Cohen, Shelby Allen, Pam Rimington, Jeannette de Beauvoir, and especially Wilderness Sarchild, who encouraged and advised me in many areas of poetry.

Many poems were paired and inspired by paintings and collages at the Cape Cod's Cultural Center as a part of Mutual Muses, organized and celebrated by Lauren Wolk: "Sippiwisset Mother," "Blue Horses," "Shootflying Hill Beckons the Mind," "The History of a Road," and "Stopping on the Bridge." Thank you, Lauren.

I am especially grateful to the Narrow Land Poets, my ongoing poetry group, who give encouragement, honest criticism, and attention to every detail: Susan Graesser, Lucile Burt, Ginia Pati, Leo Thiboult, Donna O'Connell, Margaret Rice-Moir, Margaret Phillips, Marjorie Block, Paula Erickson, the late BeeBee Pearson, and especially Chuck Madansky.

Gratitude runs deep to friends, some of whom are former students, who have been supportive and helpful over the period that I have been writing. There are many but I would like to give special thanks to Jenny Price-Smith, Kathy Braeman, Katharine Derderian, Angela Hammond, Andrew Schneider, Brian Price, Lee Roscoe, and Jane Higgins.

My family has been supportive, especially my husband Jeff Bumby who became a poet himself. My sister June has read many drafts, and given excellent advice at all stages. My other sisters Cynthia and Jackie Ashley, my brother-in-law Mike Hager, and my niece Kristen Brooks, have all been interested and helpful. My niece Ashley has been my most constant and insightful fan and critic. Thanks to my children and grandchildren for inspiring so many of these poems.

Contents

1. In the Marsh—In a Family

Arriving	17
If I Find the Right Pen	18
Sippewissett Mother	20
Rescue	22
The Courage of Boys	24
Becoming Owain	25
Aubade for the Oil Spill in Oakland, Thanksgiving, 2007	27
The Truthteller Robot	28
Found Poem: Dashiell's Five-Year-Old Christmas List for Santa	29
The World's True Blue Bloods	30
Pocasset Early Morning	31
Stopping on the Bridge	32
Giving In	33
Things on Top of the Car	34
Monday Morning Static	35
Love and Grief on June 20	36
Love in the Time of Fear	37
First Steps	38
Last Day of Nesting Season in the Marsh	39
Imprint of a Wisconsin Winter	40
Snow Writing	41
Winter Studies 2010–2011, Isle Royale, Lake Superior	42
The History of a Road	45
Cape Cod Mystic	46

2. In the Night

Animal Nights	49
Night Geography	50

The Women's House	51
Deep	53
The Baby from Another World	54
3 A.M.	56
Isabella	57
Rereading Djuna Barnes' *Nightwood*	58
"Soap Bubbles in my Eyes"	59
Edward Hopper's Cape Cod Evening	60
The Moon on the Day of Your Birth	61

3. In the World and Everywhere

Blue Horses	65
The Unknown Migrant	66
The Hills of Battir	69
Witness in Sheikh Jarrah, East Jerusalem in 2011	71
Some Advice If You Want to Go to a Peace Vigil	73
Machu Picchu	75
Pilgrimage to Race Point	76
Wow! A Baby	78
Flying Children	79
The Fast Ferry to Boston	81
Heavens for Mothers	82
April Birthday	84
Embryo	86
Two Backyards	87
Music and Sorrow	89
Our Distance Relationship	91
The Questioner	92
Strangers in the Airport, 1980	93
After the Accident	94
Saving You	96
Eritrea	97
Elder Love	98

Notes from a Volunteer Naturalist at Wellfleet Bay	100
1601 Pennsylvania Avenue	102
Refugees	104
Free and Hiding	105
Changing the Flag and Seal	106
Pansies	108
Turning Compost	110
Bury me, my children	112
Stopping on the Bridge #2	113
Kneel down	114

1. In the Marsh—In a Family

Arriving

When I arrived at destination Cape Cod
I had so many plans—
walk from the beach in Eastham
along the ocean's edge, 25 miles
to the tip of Provincetown
practice by running through the waves
from Nauset Light to Coast Guard beach.
I wanted to join a tennis team
or get a degree in nutrition
or maybe psychology.

But suddenly I knew I couldn't.

When I settled in
      I discovered as the sun was setting
      the sky turned red
      and the red spread
      from one tidal pool to the next
      making stripes of beige and fire
      on the mud flats of the bay
      and all the windows were flames.

Days I watched for hours
      a mother terrapin
      find the perfect place to dig her nest.
      Then months later out came the hatchlings—
      one day, 22 perfect hatchlings
      another time a hatchling emerged
      from an egg in the palm of my hand
      and looked up.

And slowly
    slowly
I realized this joy was enough.

If I Find the Right Pen

I am searching
for the perfect pen.

The ink must come
from two colors:
first, a mauvy rose
surrounded by a second,
a line of fiery gold.
The colors must seep
into each other's edges
yet hold their own inside.

And what
kind of printer?

Yes, a special printer.
For this poem
must be published.
Everyone must
know   see   smell
Boat Meadow Marsh
this very fall.

Feel the fertility of undercolor
which bursts through the salt-burnt
ends of the sea lavender
lies down in Spartina patens
glows in Spartina alterniflora
and seems to reach
the top of the setting sun.

The only words in my poem
will be *The Marsh*.

Then everyone who feels
the cellular truth of the ink's colors
will know.

Sippewissett Mother

Grandmother's house is a summer country.
Dark comes before we arrive.
The bridge looms like a wake-up ghost.

When I roll down the window
dark and odor flow in:
It's skunk! We're here! Cape Cod!

*Oh take me back to Sippewissett
Where the wissets sip the sea*

Tossing my geometry book
I see your note:
Get your sister up. Heat up the tater tots.

What about father?
Then I remember, he's on a trip.
And so you go behind a closed door.

*Bring me home to sweet Pocasset
Where the pokes will set us free*

We picked up shells in the tide lines,
sucked the salt in their tiny ridges.

The taste of Father's burnt hamburgers.
An upstairs door creaks open.
My older sister leaves the table.

You come out of the bedroom,
slip on the stairs. Father and I
tumble up to catch you.

*Bobby doesn't love me. He won't say
he loves me.* I beg my father,
Tell Mommy you love her.

On summer nights you sang to us, your children—
Lavender blue dilly, dilly, lavender green

You and I elbow paddled from rowboat to buoy
toes peeking out of the water.

*We will row to Nashaquitsa
passing nashas on the key*

We counted the jewels in the jetty rocks—
sparkles counted double.

*Let me bathe in Cummaquissit
With the commas on the lea*

I'm back with the wissits, Mother,
but I can't tell you.
You are gone.

*Let me cry in Willamesset
While willets sing in the marsh.*

Rescue

When Jackie was three
she bounded about the house
on all fours, like a puppy, like a colt.

Jackie and her toy horses
rode around the house turning
it into sweet grassy meadows.

At 15 Jackie earned enough to buy a horse.
She rode her horse all over town.
At night she wanted to sleep in the barn.

A horse can lead
A horse can follow
A horse can sense

Ginny, Ginny! called Jackie's father
Where was his wife?
Where was Jackie's mother?

Jackie and her horse rode out of the sadness.
She saw the world through two ears
and a black and white mane.

As an adult therapist, Jackie chose horses
to soothe and restore her clients.
Her special horse was Jinlab.

Jinlab was a rescue horse.
A five-month-old mustang
The Bureau of Land Management would not keep.

A horse can lead
A horse can follow
A horse can sense

I have named you Jinlab,
Tibetan for Wave of Grace.
You are the mover of my body.

Without touching the earth,
our spines electrify together
as we walk towards each other.

Jinlab approaches Jackie's client,
an angry, abused woman who melts
when the horse, head down, moves close.

A horse can lead
A horse can follow
A horse can sense

Jackie imagines her mother
her body wracked with pain
eased by alcohol, meeting her mustang.

Although she has been dead 40 years
Ginny knows Jini
and the other way round.

The Courage of Boys

After the bombing
of Baghdad's oldest book market
the letters are on fire
a mound of words run
sideways and books explode
like popcorn.
Men are running, screaming.
One boy stays.
He crouches on top of a knoll
of singed pages, his pants torn
his smudged face intent,
almost triumphant:
he has found one whole book.

*

At Thoreau's cairn
on Walden Pond another boy
on a fieldtrip heard something
that woke him up.
Now he won't let his buddies
see him scribble on a stone,
a message to the man of peace
of whom he knew nothing
about before today
since he didn't read the assignment.
He slips the rock down a pant leg
and warily pushes it
toward the pile with his heel.

Becoming Owain

Born at dawn in a semi-lit room,
a midnight ride in frozen January air,
a small warm body on my body.
The next day is clear as ice,
but often I remember it
                foggy with snow.

Why won't she open her eyes?
I asked the doctor
Is she blind?
He carried her to the window
Her eyes are fine.
She's not ready
        to face
                the world's light.

When she was three
I turned over a printed computer sheet.
Here, draw Megan, I said.
She turned the paper to the printed side,
drew a square with colorful dots around it.
Is that you?
That's me when I was a kite.

In the children's theatre of folktales
Megan did not want to be a princess
                or a warrior.
She wanted to be a rabbit
                or a dragon.
Rabbit Megan visited her grandfather
in the hospital at intermission
bringing a birthday cake.
His birthday was important to the bunny.

In high school
she cannot accept birthday parties
for herself—subverts the surprises.
One year enough to bring her
to the emergency room,
nothing was revealed.

Did Megan feel she was not fully born
                            not really here
until later
        name changed to Owain
                  uses male pronouns
                  rejects binary categories?

He did have two children
        breastfed both of them
                and is now central
                        to a 3-parent loving family.

Is he finally himself?
        May I celebrate his birthday now?

Aubade for the Oil Spill in Oakland, Thanksgiving, 2007

We drive together in new morning light
bringing the winning dish detergent, Dawn,
to take the oil from feathers before night.

We see the black ooze preventing their flight
puzzling at the power of blue ooze, Dawn.
We drive together in new morning light.

You are on intake using science and insight,
selecting birds that may rise from those too far gone.
You towel oil from feathers from this blight.

You are a different child driving in the dim light
who cried at the death of a worm on our lawn.
Now choose the few birds who can win this fight.

My job spreading blankets shields birds from the sight
of all eyes staring which might cause too much fright
for birds whose feathers must dry before night.

We hope that the cleaned birds will preen before flight
without oil on their feathers the birds will drown.
We drive home together in the setting light,
fearful of oil spills and earth's coming night.

The Truthteller Robot

Cyrus, age four,
carries his Halloween bucket
up to the family room
and chooses a red lollipop.
He sucks the candy and watches
an astronaut video.
Then he gets out the plastic spaceship
and various figures and one rectangular
wooden block and makes them move
to the ship.

Get in the spaceship
Going to the moon.

Okay, Captain.

Bring the flag.

The block in
robot voice says,

That's not a flag;
that's a half-eaten lollipop.

Found Poem: Dashiell's Five-Year-Old Christmas List for Santa

water bottle with a picture of Santa and a Christmas tree

sign that says "No More War"

dishwashing gloves in xs size

wonder woman spoon

travel mug (not ceramic)

Harry Potter robe, glasses, and wand

snow blower with a remote control that can be used from inside
the house for outside
and go down the steps

(tell Santa he doesn't have to bring everything)

The World's True Blue Bloods

The UPS man is shocked
coming up the walkway.
The stench makes him reel.
A teeming marsh odor dominates
spicy marigolds, subtle perfume of petunias.
He sees the large horseshoe crabs
set like royalty at the top of the path.
They and the many slipper shells and limpets
who died on their backs, deliver the strong
delicious smell of decay.

I am of the marsh
in awe of horseshoe crabs
who during the first full moon of June
crawl out of the ocean—
the females carrying the male horseshoe crabs
limpets, dog whelks, dwarf tritons
even the red knots balancing
like gymnasts on their caramel-colored backs
waiting for the glistening, gelatinous mounds
of eggs—a 400-million-year-old-ritual—
feeding hundreds of ocean creatures.
To humans they give blue blood,
detect bacteria, create vaccines
for Ebola, *for Covid-19.*
An ancient purifier of the ocean's waters
now harvested in medical labs.
Still they thrive while giving their lives
to the world and crawling
on the bottom of the sea.

Pocasset Early Morning

The small harbor is empty, the beach in shade.
No one unties a rowboat and rows to the sailboat.
No one rocks in high-backed chairs,
on porches that wrap around houses.
No one stands in the doorway

and sees what the high night tide brought—
the perfect scallop shell under the seaweed.
The first comber sees the most.
She brings the horseshoe crab back to the water
stays watching its graceful legs
swim-walk away among the minnows.
Stays awhile, feet sinking deeper and deeper,
hidden now under sand and water,
feels she will sink until water covers her,
and she will swim with the fish

until another comes
from the river side,
coffee in hand,
shatters the connection.

Stopping on the Bridge

Speeding along Bridge Road
late for a meeting,
the sky turned from blank
to blazing crimson, the sun
changed windows into fiery mirrors
turning the white bridge pink.
I ached for you to see this world—
not a picture on a cell phone
but to be here with me.

Then a Great Blue Heron
lifted its wings out of the marsh
and as it flew turned lavender.
A lavender heron!
I would have missed it if
I hadn't stopped
suddenly
illegally
on the bridge.

How is it that nature
makes the whole sad world
glow?

Giving In

I have come back to you
Again
Against the advice of friends
And professionals—
Even my own best judgment.
You make my bones weak and my nerves high.
You are the moment when
Sleep's inward warmth
Caves to the day's surprise.
You are the Call.
One hint of you in the air
And I want to live endlessly.
When I think of you
I become smooth as shiny melted chocolate
Bowls of cloves, cayenne, and cinnamon.
Winds move me
To hills of glossy green leaves
In softly rounded bushes.
I look down into the hut of your
Darkness.
I am a worm deep in the earth.
I follow swirls up to the sky;
I can see
Air.
The scent of clean water,
The sound of moving
Water mixed with fertile soil
Hints of burning wood
Aroma
I am yours,
And you are
Such sweet bitterness—
Oh, coffee!

Things on Top of the Car

Leaving the house is difficult.
There are so many things you must take with you.
Getting them down the front steps—
many don't want to be folded, zipped,
or tucked under an arm.
How do you get you and them into the car?
First you have to open the door.
Some go on the ground,
some hang on you
rolling down your arm,
and some go on top of the car.

Driving away
you realize you don't
and you won't
have them all
when the coffee spills over
the windshield and the cup clonks
against the hood
and the pieces clink in the street.

Monday Morning Static

You leave your   cough of cuppee
on the banister

Leap for the bus as it flies by

Squeeze in between two plump
people, one with a small package

Look in the package for a cup of coffee

Don't tell the man who gets up
that he's left a package

You might like it

Look around for some food
Since you left your lunch half-made

Lick the pennies you find on the floor

Don't believe the street signs
when looking for your stop

They are changed every night

Obey the sign that says
Check your feet for spiders

as you leave the bus
Gently extricate the spiders—

they belong to the Transit Authority

Love and Grief on June 20

Every year on June 20
the sun stays in the sky
longer than any other day.
Our wedding   June 20, 2015.
The short dark time follows
                     June 20, 2020
my husband and I on Cape Cod
watch his brother die through zoom
in a hospital room
                     from Covid

                     in Wisconsin.
His daughters give loving tributes,
zooming in from different lives and places
like the chorus in a Greek tragedy.
A priest with soft prayers
brings dignity and ritual.
The nurses, the protagonists,
take him off the ventilator,
hold his hand, stroke his head.
He moves slightly, and then
                     he doesn't.

Love in the Time of Fear

Take this apple from my hand,
shiny and red. Are you afraid?

Do you think it contains
knowledge of evil?   poison?   germs?

Take this cup of stinging nettles tea.
Drink it. It's for health.

Forget the apple; take my hand. I am not
Eve, not Snow White's Wicked Queen.

Forget the tea; take my lips. Experts say
touch and affection boosts immunity.

Curl your body around mine. We create
the shape of continents.

This is ancient knowledge—
love makes us strong.

First Steps

Diamondback hatchlings where are you going
under the wrack behind the dune
where the moisture clings to the bent brown grasses
and the grey tide weeds lie down like a roof?

There you will crawl on your one-inch legs
up from the wrack behind the dune
with pin-point nostrils and leathery skin
you measure moisture, you move along.

What can you see with those jet-black eyes
deep in the wrack behind the dune
where the sand is crawling with tiny creatures?
Some you will eat, or you'll be their food.

It's all a matter of size and timing,
so hide, jeweled terrapin, gain some heft.
Where will you go when the full moon tide
pours in from the ocean in powerful waves?

You must seek high ground till the tide retreats
hide in the wrack on the plateau dune,
then creep through the sand of dark encounters
with your secret story of sniff and crawl.

Last Day of Nesting Season in the Marsh

Nesting season and rain last night
makes my work easy—
deciphering animal tracks and nest sites.

No new nests, but I see
attempts by a terrapin without back legs
to nest a second time this season.

She did drop her eggs the first time—
buried by our leader.
I would make her a nest again.

There are houses and walls, a cluster
of brightly colored kayaks where
the diamond-back terrapins used to nest.

This is the last day for finding nests.
I will be back for hatchling time,
freeing 2-inch babies to make their way.

There will be a last marsh season for me—
my knees are endangered, and Indian Neck
is a long turtle trek.

Marsh dieback is real. We blamed
the purple square-backed marsh crab
which eats the Spartina grasses,

the yellow-crowned night herons for not eating
enough square-backed marsh crabs.
The overriding reason: global warming.

Imprint of a Wisconsin Winter

I follow deer prints and then see
a blur of fur, hear a twig crackle.

I touch the snow bed where she lay—
a scalloped depression with feathered edges.

I see her so clearly that
in a few years, I will think I saw her.

Another walk along an icy river, wolves
leave running tracks like knife marks.

Next year I will think I saw wolves
cavorting. This year my friend grieves

for his dead friend whom I know
only through stories and photos.

Will all winters carry the imprint
of the unseen in dust and snow?

As I grow older and forget what
I should remember, will I
remember what I never knew?

Snow Writing

I stop before a field
of new Wisconsin snow
amazed by the length and whiteness.
I want to make tracks,
let my boots sink in,
not walk on the glazed crust.

If I could write on this pure field
the trees would be capital letters
showing where to put emphasis;
the plump bushes periods
delineating ends;
falling flakes
like exclamation points;
and the smooth, thick snow
deep with possibilities.

I start out on the left-hand edge.
A tree has disrupted bark;
closer I read B.A. loves J.A.
My sister is J.A., and that romance
twenty years over.

Why should I
mark this field?
And what have I
to say to you
that I darken the page with words?
I turn back *select all*
then hit *delete*.

The thrill of the blank page again.

Winter Studies 2010–2011, Isle Royale, Lake Superior

the oldest predator/prey study in the world

The small plane must find
a patch of blue sky
to slip through
before clouds
swallow the island.

The snow screams over the ice,
bites the faces of the explorers
who can walk on its crust.
So can the wolves.

The scientists carry telemetry rods,
locate the collared wolves,
number the wolves, each one.
Enter a wolf
who stirred his observers' minds,
earned a name
not just a number.

Romeo, an upstart young male
smelling the alpha female
in her estrus moment,
can't resist her.

The pack has rules: he is repulsed.
Only the alpha male can mate in a pack.
But Chippewa Harbor Pack is safe,
a recognized territory.
Many wolves to kill moose.

Romeo races out,
finds a silky-furred female
in enemy territory,
kills a moose for her,
his first moose—his first mate.
Romeo smells other wolves.
Middle Pack is close, too close.

He speeds across the frozen marsh
leaving his kill and friend
back to the Chippewa Pack
but not for long.
He runs off again searching.
*I can just imagine
the pull of that female smell,*
the observer writes.

Winter on Isle Royale,
science bows to weather.
*Lake effect snow can turn any forecast
into a bag of lies.*
Sometimes a moist wind blurs
the boundary between lake and sky.
The explorers risk everything
for DNA samples, bones
constantly check their instruments
make wishes to the weather.

Sharp moose kicks, enemy wolves
deep snow, icy pools, starvation.
Who would list abandoned mine pits?
Romeo falls, drowns in freezing water
deep in a mine hole.

He was the alpha male
of a new pack
without enough time
to become King Romeo
of the Royal Island.

*This poem is based on *Winter Studies 2010–2011: Notes from the Field* by John A. Vucetich. The italicized phrases are direct quotes from Vucetich.

The History of a Road

Shootflying Hill Road beckons the mind.
There are more wooded paths than time to follow.
Hunters stood on the hill, crouched near the woods.
Deer, except one, disappeared in the trees.

There is more to know than time to learn,
Further to go than means to get there.
Shootflying Hill Road carried stagecoaches:
Brides to the West, caskets to the East.

Is there more to a year than spring in the woods?
Sun flecks and mud turn all early green.
Violets appear and birds claim space.
An old rock brags a new moss shawl.

More paths call us and we must choose.
We follow flagstones or animal paths.
The woods do not reach as deep as before.
Route 6 stops the growth of the forest floor.

The highway's its own path—we fly faster.
Like a giant spool the route unravels.
Too many tears for us to mend.
Every road has a fork and an end.

Cape Cod Mystic

Face the line of sky and sea
Place each foot upon the earth

Move into the water
Sink into the soil of the sea

Turn your toes into mouths
Sucking sand like food

Be the floor for scurrying crabs
The pool for Mummichogs and Sticklebacks

Bow your head to sunlight in water
Be the port for breezes moving across your face

Keep walking or start to swim
Each age of yourself will come back

Accept all selves
Imagined, former, better—all

Become a sea creature
Fit into this liquid moment

2. In the Night

Animal Nights

2 a.m.
Nursing my baby
a state of oneness
even whispering is distance
We look at each other
just as the wide-eyed
snowy owl once stared at me
Yes you   Yes us

3 a.m.
Sleeping beside my husband
gradually my breast
awakens to an enveloping molasses
dark sweetness reaches up
to the muscle in my neck and
spreads down to the bones of my ankle
and a white mare gallops by

4 a.m.
We are hibernating bears
talking asleep
Our words have humorous illogic
as we climb into each other's
dreams

6 a.m.
Waking,
I long to return to my life

Night Geography

In the glow of the candle
we touch toes to head
fingers light as winter moths.

I am in the bamboo forests in China
in tall, light swaying trees.
I leap towards you;
you catch and hold me.

We stand together on bamboo stalks.
Then you release me, and I begin
to soar. I gasp for air and sail
without boundaries. Finally I reach
the ground, and you are there.

We pause at a floating cave of water
waiting at the edge, allowing the space
between us to become electric.

The female in me
in thrall with pure dark
longs to blow out the candle,
but the male in you sees
a problem and needs light.

You solve the problem
and transport me to another land.
The light is off, candle out.
We are long,
stretching, relaxing together.
And I know this is,
of course, one meaning
of the word
love.

The Women's House

When I sleep
my mothers move about my house.
My mother's mother sparkling
the kitchen, setting her crystal apple pie
on the moist counter. No one sees her
go to bed or get up. Look,
my sister's daughter points, her
apron is growing from her shoulder blades.

My own mother hides
under the sofa. No one can coax her
out, but she giggles when we bounce
on the cushions and burps and falls asleep
without brushing her teeth.

My father's mother arrives
while I am sleeping. Her trunks
are made of porcelain. She's been
to China and to Greece visiting
herself in a former life.
She has sent my sister
on a quest to an unknown country.
I want to touch the faint mustache
of this large grandmother, but she won't
cuddle. She has exotic gifts—
all for my sister.

In the morning
I can't remember
where everyone is.
I wash my daughter's face
and so many eyes stare back—

I wonder who I am
really taking care of
and when will I see
my sister again.

Deep

I am as deep as a nylon stocking, and though you come inside me, you will never find the end. You press down gently, gently as if you are an iron who would smooth my body's wrinkles. I turn placing more of me on the board so you can reach every crease and corner. And then I turn back to get your full, smooth weight, the iron of the iron.

The Baby from Another World

In the ninth month
before my first child was born
I had three dreams.

In the first my baby was a litter of kittens—
light, fluffy fur coming through my legs—
each kitten a consummation of soft
and wiggliness. I nursed them one
after another—tiny teeth kneaded me
filling me with pleasure and fear.
I was still a woman.
Everyone wanted to see my babies.
I ran away and lived with them in the forest.

In my second dream my baby was Japanese,
and my red-haired husband was more
perplexed than angry. My mother-in-law
wept and proclaimed her love for me.
We went back to the hospital.
All the babies born that day
were Asian, said the nurse in charge.

In my third dream I carried
my baby around in a shoe box.
I had to check her in at several libraries.
I waited in line at the reference desk,
behind people with books and manuscripts.
People peered into the box and backed away.
One librarian cataloged her
Infinitesimal fingers and toes.
My baby's eyes accused me,
I'm small but complete;
stop trying to know why.

When my real baby came
we looked at each other—
her eyes were the skies from another world.

3 A.M.

When I saw you for the first time,
years and earth shifted within.
Spinning, spinning deeper, unsettling
who I was back to who I had been.

I was a new mother
holding her   my baby.
Shaking like upside down leaves
twirling to right themselves.

I entered the night space and saw
naked young skin on naked young skin.
You had moved from inside to outside,
but still my body held you.

Awe from your downcast eyes,
filled the deep night hour
when both you and I were born.
And the room shook with new feeling.

Isabella

I am barely aware of
the drama on my bed
in mid night.
I sense movement.
Then Isabella comes to me
in my dreams with
her complaint: he pushed me off.

There she is with her tiger eye make-up,
her white bib, white paws and one white
garter on her left leg, and the whorls
of chestnut red among the black stripes.

She looks at me—

*How I could have loved you
if he hadn't been here first!
I could have loved him too if
you hadn't corrupted him to
singular love—*

*Now I am looking for my one and only.
I sleep with strangers here, and some
are sweet like you,
but they always leave.*

*When I find mine, you will be
surprised—my meadow brook purr
will become a mighty falls.*

Rereading Djuna Barnes' *Nightwood*

This novel, in a night world, embraces
the dark sky as I do. The characters
contemplate the sleep of animals.
What of the great sleep of the elephant?
The fine thin sleep of the bird?
Why, as a mental somnambulist,
do I feel superior to the mass
of sleeping humanity?
How joyfully I woke at two a.m.
to nurse my baby and cherished
those moments we were awake
together with the whole world asleep.
The main character ran away from
motherhood, and yet I relate to her.
We both feel "different" and
long to be other than human.

"Soap Bubbles in my Eyes"

The children are safely asleep
an August evening in Philadelphia
when one parent rides his bike
past brick walls of crying graffiti.

tumbling, tumbling, words crack bones

The signs reek of this heartbreak summer:
ICE raids, Black lives, teeming hospitals,
a virus that destroys dreams, sickens, kills.
A message high on a building catches him.

He knows those signs of injustice.
It's the claim of a poem
he hasn't seen before.
His eyes leave the straight ahead,

tumbling, tumbling, words crack bones

and the bike hits the curb. He reads
Sometimes I feel dreamy and
Sometimes I get soap bubbles in my eyes
and hears the snap of his collar bone.

Edward Hopper's Cape Cod Evening

The door will never open.
The man will never throw the ball
because the dog has escaped
into a sea of light-touched grass.
The man is trapped by cobalt shadows.

The shadows live inside the house
claustrophobic among pillows,
coats on hooks. When
the woman and the man come out,
the blue comes with them.

The woman looms above the seated man.
Her whale white forehead and green breasts
pin him to the step. She crosses her arms,
accuses but can never ask,
Why don't you desire me?

The azure shade hovers under the door's roof.
It flows to the pine trees,
the branches on fire with her blue anger,
ebony trunks glowing with resentment.
The man's reply is the painting.

The Moon on the Day of Your Birth

When you were born
the moon shone bright in the night sky.
Your mother saw the moon as she walked to the car.
From inside it was framed in the blue rim

    of the window. That white sphere
        moved with you to the hospital, and there
        through a tiny window your mother saw it,
        and you appeared.

Years later on Cape Cod, as you walked on the bay flats
the full moon glistened in the winding marsh streams
illuminating the sea lavender and the lapel
of the red-winged blackbird.

On Great Pond in July as you sat watching,
the cratered image multiplied in the wind-ruffled waves
and the echoes of those distorted moons
called to you. You listened.

3. In the World and Everywhere

Blue Horses

There is space enough
in the belly of this horse
for me to crawl
inside and escape
the chaos of this time.

There is strength enough
for my blue horse
to travel miles to carry
my loved ones on her back
to the safety of a land
where form and color are boundaries
and fear and greed evaporate.

There is movement enough—
her tail and mane become flags—
flying for artists and poets
who carry a counter message
across space and time.

There are enough blue horses
in our world who gallop
over battlefields healing
with the mystery
of blue.

The Unknown Migrant

248,000 dead Civil War soldiers
lie unidentified. An unknowable
number from the world wars,
Korea, and Viet Nam.
A tomb on a prominent hill
in Arlington Cemetery to
The Unknown Soldier
honors all.

Tens of thousands of migrants
disappeared on their journeys.
Bodies lie at the bottom of the sea
or bleach to bones in the desert,
barely counted in life,
never registered in death.
Anonymous bodies fill the ditches.
No country wants them.
No country has a statue
The Unknown Migrant.

      *

Alone in Honduras,
husband dead, my older child kidnapped,

I was strong   strong as the willow.
Strong enough to bend, then straighten.

I took my little one
to escape the violence.
We were strong together.
We walked fast.

Not fast enough, the coyote said
We are separating the children.
They will come later.
No, I said.
This is not a choice, he said.

We arrived bruised, burnt, thirsty,
but we reached the border
the detention center   the doghouse   the ice box

coyotes   polleros   smugglers.
Where is my son   my Javier?
He will come later.
Each day I asked   *When will he come?*
They said,   *Soon.*

But there are no children here.
I marked a dot on my arm for each day.
So many dots.
What are those marks?   They are gang symbols.
Clean your arm.

I saw Christina who started with me.
Her son was not separated at the start.
He was separated here—taken to another icebox
I try to swear like Christina.
When I scream I am taken away
            —slapped into silence—
left solitary in a windowless room.

Finally, I saw him
small, black hair, brown eyes.
I called to him through the wires
Javier   Javier   my son.

He just stared at me.
A woman snapped back,
This is my son, Fernando.

I am a thing   bursting   thrown in the fire
               —finally exploding—
I am not strong.

Have I forgotten what Javier looks like?
               Is that my voice screaming?
     my mouth opens   no sound.
           My voice is lost.

               *

On the US-Mexican border 1,000 children
separated from their parents and guardians,
more than 100 under the age of five. Many lost.

---

*This poem is partially based on the short story "Everything Is Far from Here" by Cristina Henriquez, from *The New Yorker* and from *The Best American Short Stories, 2018,* edited by Roxane Gay.

The Hills of Battir

Terraced olive groves climb up the hills
white-washed houses like steps to the sky.
Everything is hills in the village of Battir.
Through the middle of the village runs
an unseen border between the two sides.
That 100-foot-high wall was scheduled to run
through the tiny, ancient village
in a formal peace plan.
The houses did not know which side to choose.
The olive trees—oldest in the world—knew—
they spoke Arabic. The Peace plan failed.
The wall only a threat.

Ramzi led the Palestinian's children's orchestra,
Al Kamandjati, on a bus from Ramallah to Battir
on rough pavement, through a tunnel,
above them the swish of Israeli cars
speeding on highways.
Palestinians in the understory

the children played to the hills of Battir.
Rasha's flute sang of her father's constant
harassment, and her anxiety melted.
Soldiers watched from towers,
machine guns aimed.

Ramzi heard the notes of flute and violin
in Battir. Music knew no borders.
He has more ambitious dreams—
imagines a train snaking through Israel
to the old villages: Na' ani, his grandfather's village,
Jenin, Arroub, Shafat, Beer-Shebah.

If they are ruins he will play to the ruins.
The oud and bazuk will drift
from the train to the soil
and the trees will become strong.
How can Ramzi love
Na'ani, call it home,
When he has never seen it?
We grew apricots and almonds,
his grandfather says proudly
who now cleans the streets
of Al Amari Refugee Camp.

Ramzi will play the bazuk and violin
to Na'ani. The children will play
to their villages which they will see
for the first time. Music in the fig trees
their grandparents' villages
reaching all the trees of the earth
awaking the people of the world,
bringing the Palestinians home.

*This poem is based on the book *Children of the Stone* by Sandy Tolan, Bloomsbury Publishing Plc. 2015.

Witness in Sheikh Jarrah, East Jerusalem in 2011

He approaches our car,
makes Hannan stop.
Like the ancient mariner,
he must tell his story.

Look at this beautiful lemon tree.
I planted it.
Look at this spacious house with rooms
for my parents
my children
my brothers and their children
my sisters
nieces, nephews
my in-laws
my grandchildren.
I built it. We all lived together here.
We were refugees from Jaffa in 1948
We were forced from a beautiful estate
with apricots and almonds.
Now we are refugees again—
26 people, 4 generations—
forced to leave our house,
our house surrounded by soldiers, guns, tanks.
For one year we lived in a tent
on the pavement in front of our house,
and in this weedy field.
We watched the small Jewish family come and go
only two adults and a baby.
We watched men erect the huge Menorah on the roof.

*Now only I am left.
I come here every day.
I built this house
for my parents, my brothers, my children,
my grandchildren.
How can I leave this lemon tree?
I planted it. How can I leave?*

Some Advice If You Want to Go to a Peace Vigil

In summer, you need to prepare
      as if you are going to the beach:
      sunblock, a hat, a chair
      (if your legs are over eighty),
      and dark glasses.

In the winter, you need to prepare
      as if you are going hunting:
      a thinsulated jacket, mittens,
      a chair for the blind,
      and dark glasses.

If you come for the first time, you may
      be stunned by others' signs.
      Their words will be fire-lighted
      jack-o-lanterns in your dreams.

Be prepared for the mother
      who will tell you that you stab her heart
      destroy the glory of her son's death.

Be dry and immovable like flowers in a press,
      not like your friend who
      when the war broke out
      checked herself into a psychiatric ward,
      cried for birds in the bombed aviary.

You may have to give up
      the belief that you create
      more peace than conflict.

Come anyway.
>	Your friend is back,
>	stands beside you,
>	wears dark glasses.

Machu Picchu

I never dreamt of Machu Picchu
Holy place of mist and stones
A valley on top of a mountain
Where once the Incas flourished.

I never dreamt of Machu Picchu
Lost civilization to the Spanish
Immune to its spell, they left it,
And there the Quechuans still pray.

Fire, earth, air, water
Mist is a mixture of water and air.
Stone the confluence of earth and fire.
Gifts to a people who worship mountains.

I never dreamt of Machu Picchu
Pacchu Mama and Templo del Sol
Spanish is not the language of Peru.
Christianity is not the religion.

I never dreamt of Machu Picchu
Simply climbed up 3,000 stairs
And down to a mother and baby llama
And to the worship of earth and air.

Pilgrimage to Race Point

April day of gray mist,
a darker gray the ocean waters,
the horizon but a smudge.
Jesse M. brings his binoculared group
in search for his favorite celebrities.

Last week he saw seven
gliding back and forth,
mouths open like giant sieves
letting water out, eating millions
of minuscule plankton.

Hunted almost to extinction
in the romantic whaling days,
they were the "Right" Whale,
the only whale that floated
easy to bring to port.

Now only 360 left in 2021;
no calves born in 2018.
Fishing gear and boat collisions
the greatest cause of death.
No whales in the fog today.

Back at the Center,
hanging above our heads
the skeleton of Spinnaker
maybe 100 feet long.
We see a rope hanging

through her mouth and nose.
The plaque says: *Spinnaker*
An inspiration to Resilience.

Four times she was entangled.
Three times the marine response

disentangled her. The fourth time
she succumbed, only 11 years old.
Jesse says, *We are lucky to be alive and*
see these marvelous creatures—
share the earth and time with them.

Wow! A Baby

Five hundred friends are celebrating!
You've arrived, barely 3 months old—
a "wee cetacean" only 3 tons
and 19 feet long,
the first right whale calf
in Cape Cod Bay this season.

Oh, Baby you've come a long way:
1200 miles swimming a water road
jammed with fishing boats with gear.
Your mother has known boat strikes;
"Millipede," the scars on her head
like a million legs, identify her.

Sweet bambino, stay in our bay,
your nursery and feeding station
safe for a mother and calf.
Aerial surveillance, "Friends of Right Whales"
Cape Cod institutions and tourists
watch over you. But you can't stay too long.

You and Millipede must swim to the cold
north waters where the plankton flourishes,
avoid the dark, underwater shadows
of lobster ropes, propellers, all fishing gear
that wraps, stabs, and tears at your flesh.
Precious pair of a dying species please
weave through these dangers
and return to us next year.

Flying Children

At sixteen I saw my baby sister fly
out of the window
riding on her teddy bear
down, down to stillness.
Afraid she had no face,
I lifted her without looking.
From soft bear fur
emerged her perfect face
with only one arm askew.
From that day I feared flying children.

When my first child climbed
to the top of our pine tree
I closed my eyes and turned
the air heavy holding her up
changed branches into jail bars.

Now grown, she is still flying
running, biking, climbing
to the top of the sky:
Mt. Washington, Slide Mountain
Cordillera Blanca Range,
next is Kilimanjaro
tallest free-standing mountain
with three sleeping volcanoes.

My second child was always
leaping, spinning, jumping—
the ground was no place for her.
At eight she flew backwards
off the swing, breaking her arm,
the same arm that held the teddy bear.
My eyes saw three broken children.

At ten, rubber bands could not
restrain her dancing hair,
her hands were always reaching
for the door top, her legs like scissors
as she darted through the house
trailing things that fell from trees.

I cannot keep these children
earthbound.
Their pact with the sky
is stronger than my prayers.

                                                              Fly!
              let them
So

The Fast Ferry to Boston

What a day in Provincetown:
E. Dickinson's molten blue sky
with sculpted clouds above the harbor,
sailboats and fishing vessels
jumping the waves in playful antics.
The water catches the sun in its lacey crests.
Everything is light, and full of light.

Pier patrol allows me to drive my daughter
and her small old dog right up to the ferry's entrance.
She hugs me to my surprise.
Thanks for being so accommodating, she says.
She is leaving after spending a month with me
though she never intended to come to Cape Cod.
And she will be coming back.

She walks carrying Javier.
I see her go to the outside deck.
Then I can't see her.
She doesn't know
I'm waiting and watching.
The ferry toots gently
and moves from the pier.

Then the ferry turns blindingly golden.
It stops. Everything stops.
The ferry levitates above the water
almost to coral-rimmed clouds.
Then it sinks down
and moves from the dock
out into the harbor.
It carries her away
and brings us together.

Heavens for Mothers

If there are any heavens my mother will (all by herself) have one. It will not be a pansy heaven nor a fragile heaven of lilies-of-the-valley but it will be a heaven of blackred roses.
—e.e. cummings

No—our mother will not
have a heaven of blackred roses
but of lilies-of-the-valley.

She was so fragile
that she could lose herself
and become a different person,
like an actor who hears
a wrong cue. She would say
*Yes, I wrote that, but
that wasn't me.*

In my parents courting days
everyone giggled at her malapropisms
and misspellings—One letter read—
*Don't worry Bobby,
I'm going on a sleigh ride,
But I won't be cold—
I'll be raped in a blanket.*
A natural ditz—acceptable
in her time. Not in her daughters'.

Our mother, the hearth of our home,
herself in many forms: turning, turning
into a kaleidoscope's surprise.
Accepting this riddle as we left
allowed us to move more easily
among love's puzzles.

Yes, our mother will have
a lily-of-the-valley heaven,
fields of fragrance
with places to hide.

April Birthday

My father turned 91 this April. Through the bars
of his walker, his legs appear spindly.

Mid-April, the trees are see-through, buds
on the ends of twigs make the edges soft.

In the morning he sits at breakfast, head in hands,
I'm so tired and I haven't done Anything.

The fiddlehead fern pushes against the seal
of soil but can't unwrap its heavy head.

He says he feels fine; when we bring him
to the doctor—does not remember the morning distress.

From a distance the branches look like feathers—
the trees look so light they might blow away.

He cannot read novels now: the end
of the sentence is too far from the beginning.

In May the trees remember how to
stretch buds into veined leaves.

My father's mantra for most questions:
I don't remember.

The crocuses open like praying fingers—
if the air turns warm they'll ascend like balloons.

I remember his sure tennis legs, his English teacher's
memory. Today, all day, I remember his pain in my stomach.

His mind and body,
April branches.

Embryo

I'm swimming in a deep, dark cave.
I'm soft and smooth and all sides
a larva, a salamander, a guppy.
You're doing nothing wrong—
the nutrients, the rest, turn over again.
I loved the marathon—
a pool of waves and deep air.

Some waves conveyed
the path ahead—
a brain-ruled life,
expectations
relationships
     control
          decline—

So   I've decided not to grow
a short ride
forever fish
swimming in your warm,
rich blood.

Two Backyards

The first, age four,
the treasure chest
the purest gifts furthest down.

STAY OUT OF THAT JUNK
STAY AWAY FROM THE BROKEN GLASS

Couldn't resist the webby dirt and shining eyes
on top, scrolled wire
underneath, a rust-eaten chair
half a doghouse—now a crawl space
things gleamed like magnets to small hands—
gold cigarette paper, a spoon, bottle caps, pennies—
everything necessary for living.

I, a child, King of the castle
where all was in order
because each was exactly
where someone or wind
or rain had left it.

The second, at age five,
the gourmet bakery and butcher shop,
three busy companions—
me, Kit, and the cat
the ground becoming pock-marked
as we dug, massing dirt, stirring water, patting
until trembling like Jell-O at their edges—
our cakes—perfect creations.
All day the cat stalked.
I stayed behind when Kit went in.

In the semi-dark I heard my mother call.
I hurried to finish,
sweet black earth filled my mouth
richer than chocolate.
Soon I would be inside the golden window,
but first I ate my cake
and wiped the smears from my mouth
as the cat cleaned bits of feather from hers.

Music and Sorrow

Think of the lace
lost in the fire
bombing of Dresden
in World War II.

Think of the old Saxon
Library on fire
sending into the air
fragments of music,

sheets with snatches of notes—
Albinoni's scrap
caught by Giazotto,
a sad Adagio.

    *

2010, my family
some from Prague
others from Virginia
gather on Green Lake, Wisconsin.

As his brother practices
the piano, Kristian, age 2,
wonders at these tame squirrels—
in Prague wild squirrels

live in forests.
He plays with a squirrel.
Later he sees his leaping
friend mangled on the road.

In tears, Kristian climbs up
to the piano, tries to make the keys
cry for the squirrel.
His brother tells him to stop.

      *

A string quartet arrives.
They play Albioni's mournful
Adagio, requested by
the family who was touched

through their reading of
The Cellist of Sarajevo.
When the quartet finishes
Kristian, from his mother's lap

cries in a stream of Czech.
His mother translates,
Kristian thanks you for playing
the song for the dead squirrel.

Our Distance Relationship

So, we go to our separate closed domains
alone time in a shared weekend,
I to a cozy loft,
you to sun flooded windows.
You practice your violin,
I write.

You cannot stay away.
Twenty times you interrupt me—
I must share this with you.
Do you remember when . . .
or the pull of physical strings.

And yet, isn't this what I want,
another energy strong enough
to pull me out of myself?

I who am contained enough
to be alone for days
happy with the bank of snow
against the door,
I circle the tree rings inside my body,
a timeless, weatherless traveler.
You bring me back.

Oh bring me back!

The Questioner

for Kathy Derderian

Until you asked
I never thought
what part of me
would be the same
if I were born another sex
or in another century.

I have a space within
that is quiet, a slow rhythm
mesmerized by your gentle
brown eyes, and flecks
of dust in sunlight—
a delicious stillness.

Until you asked for
my free period so we
could write poetry,
I did not think I could
write and teach at the same time.
If I ignore clocks,
the flashing digitals of
cell phones, I pay,
bruised by the yells
of those who think
I don't care.

When I give up my slow
waking, I will leave—partially
because of your questions—
this pace, somewhere
in some form
loving you.

Strangers in the Airport, 1980

She walks ahead,
high heels, gold wedding band
cream-colored silk blouse.

He trails after her,
heavy, red-faced,
sweating in an ill-fitting suit.

Same gold ring.
Flops into a seat
at the gate for flight 119.

Her face tense, scans
those emerging from
the dark bridge into the bright day.

His eyes are on her.
Then he looks out the window,
then back at her, anxious.

The girl comes off the plane—
scowling, purple hair, pierced eyebrow,
same slim legs in same tight jeans.

The woman sees her,
moves quickly to embrace.
The man's face relaxes.

I see three faces transformed.

After the Accident

After the accident
the pain started in
her spine, flared out
white hot as the noon sun,
rolled down her legs
like glowing lava
from an exploding
volcano, reached
like air moving
into the pockets
around her eyes,
like earth worms
spiraling in the soil.

My sister serenely
wished for death:
hassles for her beloved,
months of therapy,
medical expenses
(that could send all the girls
in Nepal to school).

Her house is carefully
in order. She has made
amends and is loved.

We had promised
to help each other die
if the circumstances
seemed right.

A serious promise.

I am the baby sister
in awe of how she could talk.
I am the big sister
protecting her from the world's
dragons with my doll's broom.

In this moment
I am just a sister
(maybe all sisters)
and with her husband
pray for her to fight.

Now, she stands tall,
gracefully walks
like a model
on the runway
lightly holding
her walker.

Saving You

I found a group for you in St. Peter's church basement.
When you enter, one man gets a pillow for the metal chair.
They smile at you, and you smile back.
I know you like to please people.
You gave up smoking for the therapy group.
Everyone in this group has the same problem.
They say their names, and they name the problem.
They say it, and you can also say it.
You feel like laughing and crying.
You hide your face in your hands.
You could not even whisper it to us, your family.
When you go home and peel the potatoes,
      you feel different.

My younger sister plays with plastic horses.
She has her horses carry you into the sky.
She thinks everyone will be happy riding a horse.
Later when she has her own horse,
she asks you to ride it.
You are not scared even with your lacey bones.
Your daughter knows,
the horse knows:
You will not fall off.

Eritrea

I thought I'd be back to see you

Alem, Mebratoum, Hailemariam, Abdalla,
dance and pray and eat at your weddings,
hold your children and show you mine.
I wanted to remember the dignity
of your formal manners
standing barefoot
in thin clothes,
hear the name
of your town
Senafe.

I thought I'd be back to see

the rock mountains and the canyons stretching beyond,
both smeared with rouge by the lowering sun
all behind the white-washed compound
where carnations and lilies grew
for thirteen months of spring
in the Coptic calendar
and where I lived
for two years.

I always thought I'd be back.

I never thought the reserved hostility in the capitol
would prophesize the close of the US army base
and interrupt our sweet world of learning
and two mountain countries—
so similar—would begin
an endless war.

I always thought I'd be back.

Elder Love

They lived next door in senior housing
talked together at the kitchen table
hugged under the dangling light

Then the year of nights together started
He made her eggs and bacon for breakfast
She made garden burgers and kale chips for supper

They had a Christmas tree of the month
with glass test tubes of roses in June
Though they lived next door, he mailed her cards

He had faults: said he was an Air Force pilot
and a Navy Seal. There was a seal on a paperweight
on his Navy desk and he did fly model airplanes

His daughters protested; brought in nurses
She was to stay away, no calls
Then the year of nights together stopped

His last day she worked at the polls
Their mutual neighbor came with her grandson
so they could all have lunch together

He held her hand and his last remaining
model plane which the boy stared at
eyes as big as cucumber slices

He gave the boy the plane
now he had a hand free for pizza
They all laughed together

He went home for a nap; she back to the polls
Later she saw his lights were still on
found the door ajar

He was slumped on the bed
She sat next to him
held a barely warm hand

She hummed their favorite waltz
said the serenity prayer and left
quietly shutting the door

Notes from a Volunteer Naturalist at Wellfleet Bay

1.
In spring,
a ballerina who extends
her fingers in an oval
above her head is almost
as graceful as the way the
longest vines of the cat
briar lifts to the sky, divides
and curves back, making a heart
frame around its new bud.

2.
In July,
A five-year-old cried
that a fiddler crab had
pinched her. *It really,
really hurt. It hurt so-o
much. But I didn't have
to go to the hospital and
I didn't have to give up
our trip for ice cream*

3.
A nine-year-old saw a painted
turtle skip across the path from
Silver Spring to the marsh.
*Look at that turtle go. It's so fast.
That's a cheetah turtle.*

4.
It's August and soon
the groundnut vine will flower.
A mauve wash over pink petals
with chocolate centers
in tight clusters. We are all
waiting for this luscious vine
to make its sunset in the marsh.

1601 Pennsylvania Avenue

There you stand wrinkled and old
in three headdresses and a necklace of political buttons.
You seem dwarfed standing between big signs:
"No war" and "Live by the Bomb, Die by the Bomb."

There you have stood for three decades—
your only shelter an open tarp tied
to the White House's wrought iron fence—
closest neighbor to five presidents.

Dismissed by most, called daft
or insane for protesting a nuclear arsenal
that can annihilate the earth
ten times over.

Since then I have known dismissal
as I vigiled for hopeless causes
with home-made signs,
tattered flags.

I look again at your photo.
On your head, a wig—a disguise?
Over the wig a helmet—for your protection
or to honor soldiers who have died?

Over the wig and helmet, a scarf—
patterned in blue, red, and yellow flowers—
for immigrants from Mexico? from Nigeria?
from anywhere.

I see your shelter—that open tarp
held up, held down against that fence, a wall
of stability and separation
but no defense against D.C.'s August heat.

Another picture, your no-home home
surrounded by snow. (I have waved a flag
in bitter cold but always had
a warm place to go.)

Now you are gone and who knows
whom you touched. Your name
an anti-war chant: Concepcion,
Concepcion Picciotto.

Refugees

We are a stranded people

Fleeing one government, then another
fleeing poverty, disease, drought, floods

We are a forgotten people

On the edge of the water forever
the Rio Grande, the Euphrates, the Black Sea

We have been on the edge
weighted down by all we carry

We had strength once and determination
Some of us are still steel

Most of us are waiting by the water
We have dropped everything

In the distance we see trucks, boats
Two people struggle to reach a boat

They have been trying for a long time
Does the boat move farther away?

We are a waiting, dying people

We have left our culture, our language
our sick, and our old

We don't know who we are

Free and Hiding

Breaking away from your marriage
the same time your children fledge,
you wonder, for a moment, why no tears.

You move to a new place
where you have always been,
walk in the mud flats, see the periwinkles
gurgle and glide together.
And then you become tiny and safe
in an ink purple village.

Now you slip inside the fiddler crab's hole,
the scrupulously clean
one for mating and sleeping.
Ah, mud comfort—wet and soft.
You crawl into the smooth conch's
slope sliding back and forth
along the shell's spiral.
You feel dizzy, but it's fun.
You emerge from the dark
and see the sky.

You were always this animal.

Changing the Flag and Seal

How long have we waited?
How long have First Nations people waited?
How long have all the people of Massachusetts waited
with the weight of the white supremist seal
with the weight of that hate-filled flag
waving our genocides out for the world to see
waving the ways of violence
as the chosen path of life for citizens of our state?

We have waited too long.

How peaceful the sky-blue background looks.
How central the Indian in the center.
There is no peace in this deceptive flag,
and the Indian is false—his proportions
taken from a skeleton, his features
from a photograph of an Ojibwa chief in Montana.
As if all Indians in Massachusetts were dead.

We have waited too long.

The broadsword brandished above the head
of the artificial Indian shows Miles Standish's sword
ready to slaughter the Indian. Miles Standish
who ambushed and massacred the Massachusetts nation.

A commission is created to change the flag and seal.

A new design. A new era. The motto on the dying flag
in Latin begins: "By the sword we seek peace . . ."
We do not believe in the sword—in violence
against the original people who saw the light first,
in violence against any people.

Let there be a new motto
in a language we understand and speak.
Let it proclaim our aspiring values:
for all the people of Massachusetts.

Pansies

Turned inside out
their bright colors muted
the pansies lie on a mound
of loose garden dirt.
Not rich in dark minerals
nor tawny like beach sand,
it's dead-oak leaf color,
turned up, disturbed.

A few friends tossed these pansies
here three days ago. Now they lie
curled petal ropes, more the color
of the soil than their own.

And I have brought
three more pansies.
Laid them just here.
One a deep maroon velvet,
one yellow like the Goldfinch
on the rim of the bird bath
who flew away when I came out.

And one pure white,
whiter than the many daisies
growing nearby, whiter than
the bleached clam shell on the edge,
whiter than my sister's car.

But not whiter than the coat
of my newly buried cat
who kept his fur so clean
I could lick it.

He spent his time
lapping the dust from his body
until his only act was trying to breathe.

Turning Compost

Carrot peels,
eggshells, lettuce
leaves, pansy
petals, transform
into the darkest moist
soil in my compost bin.
All summer and fall
  my daughter turned
    the bin this way
      and that, delighting
        in building
          muscles. Now
            here—a spaghetti of
            mauvy-brown
          worms, wiggling
          tubes of nutrients
        creating, then
      aerating the soil.
    In spring I will
  spread this layer
out to receive
  the seeds of
    becoming. When
      I die I hope
        to give myself
          to these amazing
            animals and
          morph into
          worms. I will
        have come,
        many years
        ago, from rocky
      dust to earthy
    wriggles with a

fleeting but
stellar time
as a human creature.

Bury me, my children

in the rain
because mud
is what I want to be.

Let me become
what first crept from water,
a one-celled creature
that grew through dividing
before the time
of complex mating.

Bend over and taste
the earth and water of my grave
and be a part of an old beginning
as well as a new ending.

Drop acorns and pinecones
toss any wild seed
into the puddles of my grave
and then speak this prayer—

creep down roots
pierce my skin
sip my blood
grow up shoots
unwrap leaves in the air
eat me worms and insects
transform me
into new wild biology.

Stopping on the Bridge #2

If my soul stops
on this bridge
what is on either side?
I know only rich brown soil
that I will go to,
but there must be
a longer, deeper stream
in both directions
that flows under the bridge.
So many beliefs of what
each side is made of.
All credible. All incredible.
Yet the bridge
may be the only time
the soul gets to know
and choose. What does it know?
That the bridge is finite.
Terrible. But there is
an element of choice.

Kneel down

I will go out into the marsh
as I have done forever
and bend down to my feet
where mudsand comes through
toes like the surprise of a pop-up
picture. I crouch to tiny shells,
lick their salty ridges—daily nourishment.
Then I stand up so I am in open
sky and see an osprey fly overhead.
She is in the clouds and sun, and I
stretch up to be with her. I can feel
the high salt-grained wind.
Then I kneel down because
a small crab is climbing over the top
of my foot. I watch him crawl
and pray to this creature:

Thank you.
I will remember the tickle
of your claws and how
you changed me into just
the floor of your world.

About the Author

Dianne Woods Ashley lives a woodsy ten-minute walk to Cape Cod Bay. Dianne's poems come partly from her experiences as a volunteer at Wellfleet Bay Audubon Sanctuary, where she indulges her delight in the marsh, the water, and the woods. Her justice work on behalf of people, animals, and the earth inspire poems also.

She has received awards for her poetry from the Tony Hoagland National Poetry Competition at the Cape Cod Cultural Center, the Veterans for Peace Poetry Competition, the WOMR Joe Gouveia Regional Poetry Competition, and the *Passager* poetry contest issue. Her poems have been published in the *Cape Cod Times,* the anthology *World of Water, World of Sand,* and the national collection *Poets Against the War.*

Dianne taught English and Literary Magazine at Yorktown High School in Arlington, Virginia, and before that at Penn State, and in the Peace Corps in the rural middle school in Senafe, Eritrea. She lives in Eastham with her husband Jeff Bumby and two kittens. She has a beloved extended family including two children and two grandsons.

www.ingramcontent.com/pod-product-compliance
Lightning Source LLC
Chambersburg PA
CBHW030906170426
43193CB00009BA/751